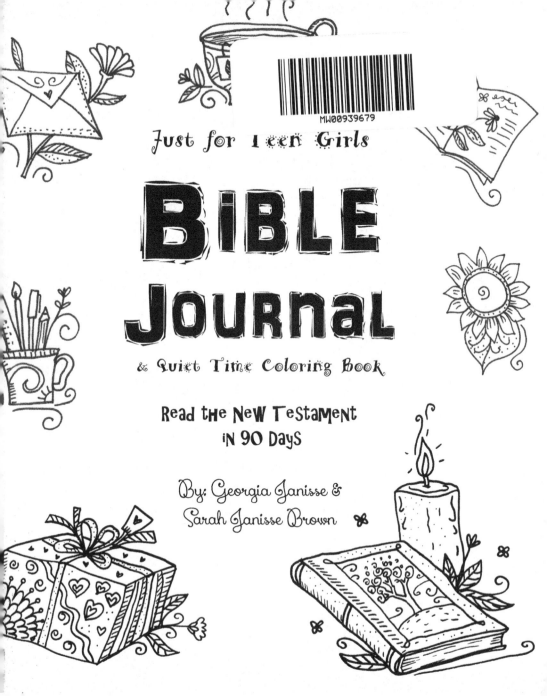

Just for Teen Girls

BIBLE
JOURNAL

& Quiet Time Coloring Book

Read the New Testament in 90 Days

By: Georgia Janisse &
Sarah Janisse Brown

This Book is
Brought to you by:

The
Thinking
Tree

Publishing Company
Made in the USA

Name:

Date:

My Bible Reading Plan - Part 1
Read Through the New Testament in 90 Days

1. Matthew 1, Romans 1-2
2. Matthew 2-3, Romans 3
3. Matthew 4-5, Romans 4
4. Matthew 6, Romans 5-6
5. Matthew 7, Romans 7
6. Matthew 8-9, Romans 8
7. Matthew 10-11, Romans 9
8. Matthew 12, Romans 10-11
9. Matthew 13, Romans 12
10. Matthew 14-15, Romans 13
11. Matthew 16-17, Romans 14
12. Matthew 18, Romans 15-16
13. Matthew 19-20, 1 Corinthians 1
14. Matthew 21-22, 1 Corinthians 2
15. Matthew 23-24, 1 Corinthians 3
16. Matthew 25, 1 Corinthians 4-5
17. Matthew 26, 1 Corinthians 6-7
18. Matthew 27-28
19. Matthew 1-2, 1 Corinthians 8
20. Matthew 3-4, 1 Corinthians 9
21. Matthew 5, 1 Corinthians 10
22. Matthew 6, 1 Corinthians 11
23. Mark 7-8, 1 Corinthians 12
24. Mark 9-10, 1 Corinthians 13
25. Mark 11-12, 1 Corinthians 14
26. Mark 13-14
27. Mark 15, 1 Corinthians 15
28. Mark 16, 1 Corinthians 16
29. Luke 1, 2 Corinthians 1
30. Luke 2, 2 Corinthians 2-3
31. Luke 3, 2 Corinthians 4-5
32. Luke 4, 2 Corinthians 6-7
33. Luke 5, 2 Corinthians 8-9
34. Luke 6, 2 Corinthians 10-11
35. Luke 7, 2 Corinthians 12-13
36. Luke 8, Galatians 1-2
37. Luke 9-10, Galatians 3
38. Luke 11-12, Galatians 4
39. Luke 13-14, Galatians 5
40. Luke 15-16, Galatians 6
41. Luke 17-18, Ephesians 1
42. Luke 19, Ephesians 2-3
43. Luke 20-21, Ephesians 4
44. Luke 22, Ephesians 5-6

My Bible Reading Plan - Part 2

Read Through the New Testament in 90 Days

45. Luke 23, Philippians 1-2

46. Luke 24, Philippians 3-4

47. John 1, Colossians 1

48. John 2-3, Colossians 2

49. John 4-5, Colossians 3

50. John 6-7, Colossians 4

51. John 8, 1 Thessalonians 1-2

52. John 9-10, 1 Thessalonians 3

53. John 11-12, 1 Thessalonians 4

54. John 13-14, 1 Thessalonians 5

55. John 15, 2 Thessalonians 1-2

56. John 16, 1 Thessalonians 3

57. John 17, 1 Timothy 1-2

58. John 18, 1 Timothy 3-4

59. John 19, 1 Timothy 5-6

60. John 20, 2 Timothy 1-2

61. John 21, 2 Timothy 3-4

62. Acts 1-2, Titus 1

63. Acts 3, Titus 2-3

64. Acts 4-5, Philemon

65. Acts 6-7, Hebrews 1

66. Acts 8, Hebrews 2-3

67. Acts 9, Hebrews 4-5

68. Acts 10-11, Hebrews 6

69. Acts 12, Hebrews 7-8

70. Acts 13-14, Hebrews 9

71. Acts 15-16, Hebrews 10

72. Acts 17-18, Hebrews 11

73. Acts 19, Hebrews 12-13

74. Acts 20, James 1-2

75. Acts 21-22, James 3

76. Acts 23-24, James 4

77. Acts 25-26, James 5

78. Acts 27, 1 Peter 1-2

79. Acts 28, 1 Peter 3-4

80. Revelation 1-2, 1 Peter 5

81. Revelation 3-4, 2 Peter 1

82. Revelation 5-6, 2 Peter 2

83. Revelation 7-8, 2 Peter 3

84. Revelation 9-10, 1 John 1

85. Revelation 11-12, 1 John 2

86. Revelation 13-14, 1 John 3

87. Revelation 15-16, 1 John 4-5

88. Revelation 17-18, 2 John

89. Revelation 19-20, 3 John

90. Revelation 21-22, Jude

Quiet time in God's word is like spending time with a friend, or reading a love letter.

Read the
**Bible
Everyday!**

Start each day
by reading the
inspirational verse.

Pray for God's
blessings as you
read His Word.

Copy
a Bible verse
into your journal.

Find a cozy place. Turn on your favorite worship music. Make a cup of tea. Relax and enjoy spending time with Jesus.

How to Choose What to Read:

You can use the "Read the New Testament in 90 Days" plan in the beginning of this journal.

OR, choose a book of the Bible, get a bookmark and read each day starting from where you left off.

If you skip a day, don't give up!

AS you color pray aNd tHiNk abOut WHat you read iN tHe BibLe today.

End of week action page and coloring page!

Write down what God showed you in His Word today.
Then, write out your prayer, or about your day or your plans.

Begin your Quiet Time with Prayer

Trust in the LORD with all your heart,
and lean not on your own understanding;
In all your ways acknowledge Him,
and He shall direct your paths.

Proverbs 3:5-6

My Bible Reading Plan for Today: _____

date: _____

A verse that touched my heart:

_____

_____

_____

_____

_____

_____

_____

_____

_____

it's Bible Reading Time!

What God Showed to Me in His Word Today:

A promise to believe,
a warning to heed, a command to obey,
encouragement to receive,
or wisdom to understand.

My Prayer

My Day

My Plans

Begin your Quiet Time with Prayer

For God so loved the world
that He gave His only begotten Son,
that whoever believes in Him should not perish
but have everlasting life.

John 3:16

My Bible Reading Plan for Today: _____

date: _____

A verse that touched my heart:

_____

_____

_____

_____

_____

_____

_____

_____

it's Bible Reading Time!

What God Showed to Me in His Word Today:

A promise to believe,
a warning to heed, a command to obey,
encouragement to receive,
or wisdom to understand.

_____

_____

_____

_____

_____

_____

_____

_____

_____

_____

My Prayer _____

_____

_____

My Day _____

_____

My Plans _____

_____

Begin your Quiet Time with Prayer

Call to Me, and I will answer you,
and show you great and mighty things,
which you do not know.

Jeremiah 33:3

My Bible Reading Plan for Today: _____

date: _____

A verse that touched my heart:

it's Bible Reading Time!

What God Showed to Me in His Word Today:

A promise to believe,
a warning to heed, a command to obey,
encouragement to receive,
or wisdom to understand.

My Prayer

My Day

My Plans

Begin your Quiet Time with Prayer

Casting all your care upon Him,

for He cares for you.

1 Peter 5:7

My Bible Reading Plan for Today: _____

date: _____

A verse that touched my heart:

it's Bible Reading Time!

What God Showed to Me in His Word Today:

A promise to believe,
a warning to heed, a command to obey,
encouragement to receive,
or wisdom to understand.

_____

_____

_____

_____

_____

_____

_____

_____

_____

My Prayer _____

_____

My Day _____

_____

My Plans _____

_____

Begin your Quiet Time with Prayer

Your word *is* a lamp to my feet
and a light to my path.
Psalm 119:105

My Bible Reading Plan for Today: _____

              date: _____

A verse that touched my heart:

_____

_____

_____

_____

_____

_____

_____

_____

it's Bible Reading Time!

What God Showed to Me in His Word Today:

A promise to believe,
a warning to heed, a command to obey,
encouragement to receive,
or wisdom to understand.

My Prayer

My Day

My Plans

Begin your Quiet Time with Prayer

He who dwells in the secret place of the Most High
Shall abide under the shadow of the Almighty.
Psalm 91:1

My Bible Reading Plan for Today: _____

date: _____

A verse that touched my heart:

_____

_____

_____

_____

_____

_____

_____

_____

it's Bible Reading Time!

What God Showed to Me in His Word Today:

A promise to believe,
a warning to heed, a command to obey,
encouragement to receive,
or wisdom to understand.

My Prayer

My Day

My Plans

Begin your Quiet Time with Prayer

The LORD *is* good,

A stronghold in the day of trouble;

And He knows those who trust in Him.

Nahum 1:7

My Bible Reading Plan for Today: _____

date: _____

A verse that touched my heart:

it's Bible Reading Time!

What God Showed to Me in His Word Today:

A promise to believe,
a warning to heed, a command to obey,
encouragement to receive,
or wisdom to understand.

My Prayer

My Day

My Plans

Four things to be thankful for:

Begin your Quiet Time with Prayer

Let the wicked forsake his way,
And the unrighteous man his thoughts;
Let him return to the LORD,
And He will have mercy on him;
And to our God, For He will abundantly pardon.

Isaiah 55:7

My Bible Reading Plan for Today: _____

date: _____

A verse that touched my heart:

it's Bible Reading Time!

What God Showed to Me in His Word Today:

A promise to believe,
a warning to heed, a command to obey,
encouragement to receive,
or wisdom to understand.

My Prayer

My Day

My Plans

Begin your Quiet Time with Prayer

But above all these things
put on love,
which is the bond of perfection.
Colossians 3:14

My Bible Reading Plan for Today: _____

date: _____

A verse that touched my heart:

it's Bible Reading Time!

What God Showed to Me in His Word Today:

A promise to believe,
a warning to heed, a command to obey,
encouragement to receive,
or wisdom to understand.

My Prayer

My Day

My Plans

Begin your Quiet Time with Prayer

For I know the thoughts that I think toward you,
says the LORD, thoughts of peace and not of evil,
to give you a future and a hope.
Jeremiah 29:11

My Bible Reading Plan for Today: _____

date: _____

A verse that touched my heart:

_____

_____

_____

_____

_____

_____

_____

_____

_____

_____

it's Bible Reading Time!

What God Showed to Me in His Word Today:

A promise to believe,
a warning to heed, a command to obey,
encouragement to receive,
or wisdom to understand.

My Prayer

My Day

My Plans

Begin your Quiet Time with Prayer

Then Jesus spoke to them again, saying,

"I am the light of the world.

He who follows Me shall not walk in darkness,

but have the light of life."

John 8:12

My Bible Reading Plan for Today: _____

date: _____

A verse that touched my heart:

_____

_____

_____

_____

_____

_____

_____

_____

_____

_____

It's Bible Reading Time!

What God Showed to Me in His Word Today:

A promise to believe,
a warning to heed, a command to obey,
encouragement to receive,
or wisdom to understand.

My Prayer

My Day

My Plans

Begin your Quiet Time with Prayer

These things I have spoken to you,
that My joy may remain in you, and that
your joy may be full.
John 15:11

My Bible Reading Plan for Today: _____

date: _____

A verse that touched my heart:

it's Bible Reading Time!

What God Showed to Me in His Word Today:

A promise to believe,
a warning to heed, a command to obey,
encouragement to receive,
or wisdom to understand.

My Prayer

My Day

My Plans

Begin your Quiet Time with Prayer

Ah, Lord God! Behold,
You have made the heavens and the earth
by Your great power and outstretched arm.
There is nothing too hard for You.
Jeremiah 32:17

My Bible Reading Plan for Today: _____
date: _____

A verse that touched my heart:

_____

_____

_____

_____

_____

_____

_____

_____

_____

it's Bible Reading Time!

What God Showed to Me in His Word Today

A promise to believe,
a warning to heed, a command to obey,
encouragement to receive,
or wisdom to understand.

_____

_____

_____

_____

_____

_____

_____

_____

My Prayer

_____

_____

My Day

_____

_____

My Plans

_____

_____

Begin your Quiet Time With Prayer

For My thoughts are not your thoughts,
Nor are your ways My ways, says the LORD.
For as the heavens are higher than the earth,
So are My ways higher than your ways,
And My thoughts than your thoughts
Isaiah 55:8-9

My Bible Reading Plan for Today: _____

date: _____

A verse that touched my heart:

it's Bible Reading Time!

What God Showed to Me in His Word Today:

A promise to believe,
a warning to heed, a command to obey,
encouragement to receive,
or wisdom to understand.

_____

_____

_____

_____

_____

_____

_____

_____

My Prayer _____

_____

My Day _____

_____

My Plans _____

_____

Four prayer requests:

Begin your Quiet Time with Prayer

And this is the will of Him who sent Me,
that everyone who sees the Son and believes in Him
may have everlasting life;
and I will raise him up at the last day.
John 6:40

My Bible Reading Plan for Today: _____

date: _____

A verse that touched my heart:

it's Bible Reading Time!

What God Showed to Me in His Word Today:

A promise to believe,
a warning to heed, a command to obey,
encouragement to receive,
or wisdom to understand.

My Prayer

My Day

My Plans

Begin your Quiet Time with Prayer

Cause me to hear Your loving-kindness in the morning,
For in You do I trust;
Cause me to know the way in which I should walk,
For I lift up my soul to You.
Psalm 143:8

My Bible Reading Plan for Today: _____

date: _____

A verse that touched my heart:

it's Bible Reading Time!

What God Showed to Me in His Word Today:

A promise to believe,
a warning to heed, a command to obey,
encouragement to receive,
or wisdom to understand.

My Prayer

My Day

My Plans

Begin your Quiet Time with Prayer

When you pass through the waters, I will be with you;
And through the rivers, they shall not overflow you.
When you walk through the fire, you shall not be burned,
Nor shall the flame scorch you.
Isaiah 43:2

My Bible Reading Plan for Today: _____

date: _____

A verse that touched my heart:

_____
_____
_____
_____
_____
_____
_____
_____
_____
_____

it's Bible Reading Time!

What God Showed to Me in His Word Today:

A promise to believe,
a warning to heed, a command to obey,
encouragement to receive,
or wisdom to understand.

_____
_____
_____
_____
_____
_____
_____
_____

My Prayer
_____
_____

My Day
_____
_____

My Plans
_____
_____

Begin your Quiet Time with Prayer

All we like sheep have gone astray;
We have turned, every one, to his own way;
And the LORD has laid on Him the iniquity of us all.
Isaiah 53:6

My Bible Reading Plan for Today: _____

date: _____

A verse that touched my heart:

it's Bible Reading Time!

What God Showed to Me in His Word Today:

A promise to believe,
a warning to heed, a command to obey,
encouragement to receive,
or wisdom to understand.

My Prayer

My Day

My Plans

Begin your Quiet Time with Prayer

He has delivered us
from the power of darkness and
conveyed us into the kingdom of the Son of His love.
Colossians 1:13

My Bible Reading Plan for Today: _____

date: _____

A verse that touched my heart:

It's Bible Reading Time!

What God Showed to Me in His Word Today:

A promise to believe,
a warning to heed, a command to obey,
encouragement to receive,
or wisdom to understand.

My Prayer

My Day

My Plans

Begin your Quiet Time with Prayer

For You, Lord, are good,
and ready to forgive,
And abundant in mercy
to all those who call upon You.
Psalm 86:5

My Bible Reading Plan for Today: _____

date: _____

A verse that touched my heart:

it's Bible Reading Time!

What God Showed to Me in His Word Today:

A promise to believe,
a warning to heed, a command to obey,
encouragement to receive,
or wisdom to understand.

My Prayer

My Day

My Plans

Begin your Quiet Time with Prayer

The LORD your God in your midst,
The Mighty One, will save;
He will rejoice over you with gladness,
He will quiet you with His love,
He will rejoice over you with singing.
Zephaniah 3:17

My Bible Reading Plan for Today: _____

date: _____

A verse that touched my heart:

_____

_____

_____

_____

_____

_____

_____

_____

_____

_____

it's Bible Reading Time!

What God Showed to Me in His Word Today:

A promise to believe,
a warning to heed, a command to obey,
encouragement to receive,
or wisdom to understand.

_____

_____

_____

_____

_____

_____

_____

_____

_____

My Prayer

_____

_____

_____

My Day

_____

_____

My Plans

_____

_____

Four goals for next week:

Begin your Quiet Time with Prayer

Be anxious for nothing, but in everything by prayer
and supplication, with thanksgiving,
let your requests be made known to God;
and the peace of God, which surpasses all understanding,
will guard your hearts and minds through Christ Jesus.

Philippians 4:6-7

My Bible Reading Plan for Today: _____

date: _____

A verse that touched my heart:

it's Bible Reading Time!

What God Showed to Me in His Word Today:

A promise to believe,
a warning to heed, a command to obey,
encouragement to receive,
or wisdom to understand.

My Prayer

My Day

My Plans

Begin your Quiet Time with Prayer

Jesus said to her,

"Did I not say to you that if you would believe

you would see the glory of God?"

John 11:40

My Bible Reading Plan for Today: _____

date: _____

A verse that touched my heart:

it's Bible Reading Time!

What God Showed to Me in His Word Today:

A promise to believe,
a warning to heed, a command to obey,
encouragement to receive,
or wisdom to understand.

My Prayer

My Day

My Plans

Begin your Quiet Time with Prayer

By this all will know
that you are My disciples,
if you have love for one another.
John 13:35

My Bible Reading Plan for Today: _____

date: _____

A verse that touched my heart:

_____
_____
_____
_____
_____
_____
_____
_____

it's Bible Reading Time!

What God Showed to Me in His Word Today:

A promise to believe,
a warning to heed, a command to obey,
encouragement to receive,
or wisdom to understand.

My Prayer

My Day

My Plans

Begin your Quiet Time with Prayer

For I, the LORD your God, will hold your right hand,
Saying to you, 'Fear not, I will help you.'
Isaiah 41:13

My Bible Reading Plan for Today: _____

date: _____

A verse that touched my heart:

_____

_____

_____

_____

_____

it's Bible Reading Time!

What God Showed to Me in His Word Today:

A promise to believe,
a warning to heed, a command to obey,
encouragement to receive,
or wisdom to understand.

My Prayer

My Day

My Plans

Begin your Quiet Time with Prayer

The LORD *is* my light and my salvation;
Whom shall I fear?
The LORD *is* the strength of my life;
Of whom shall I be afraid?
Psalm 27:1

My Bible Reading Plan for Today: _____

date: _____

A verse that touched my heart:

_____

_____

_____

_____

_____

It's Bible Reading Time!

What God Showed to Me in His Word Today:

A promise to believe,
a warning to heed, a command to obey,
encouragement to receive,
or wisdom to understand.

My Prayer

My Day

My Plans

Begin your Quiet Time with Prayer

Bearing with one another, and forgiving one another,
If anyone has a complaint against another;
even as Christ forgave you, so you also *must do.*
Colossians 3:13

My Bible Reading Plan for Today: _____

date: _____

A verse that touched my heart:

_____

_____

_____

_____

_____

_____

_____

_____

_____

it's Bible Reading Time!

What God Showed to Me in His Word Today:

A promise to believe,
a warning to heed, a command to obey,
encouragement to receive,
or wisdom to understand.

My Prayer

My Day

My Plans

Begin your Quiet Time with Prayer

If then you were raised with Christ,
seek those things which are above,
where Christ is, sitting at the right hand of God.
Colossians 3:1

My Bible Reading Plan for Today: _____

date: _____

A verse that touched my heart:

_____

_____

_____

_____

_____

_____

_____

_____

_____

it's Bible Reading Time!

What God Showed to Me in His Word Today:

A promise to believe,
a warning to heed, a command to obey,
encouragement to receive,
or wisdom to understand.

My Prayer

My Day

My Plans

Four reasons to praise God:

Begin your Quiet Time with Prayer

I will praise You,

O LORD, with my whole heart;

I will tell of all Your marvelous works.

Psalm 9:1

My Bible Reading Plan for Today: _____

date: _____

A verse that touched my heart:

_____

_____

_____

_____

_____

_____

_____

_____

_____

it's Bible Reading Time!

What God Showed to Me in His Word Today:

A promise to believe,
a warning to heed, a command to obey,
encouragement to receive,
or wisdom to understand.

My Prayer

My Day

My Plans

Begin your Quiet Time with Prayer

Being confident of this very thing,
that He who has begun a good work in you will complete it until
the day of Jesus Christ
Philippians 1:6

My Bible Reading Plan for Today: _____

date: _____

A verse that touched my heart:

_____

_____

_____

_____

_____

_____

_____

_____

_____

it's Bible Reading Time!

What God Showed to Me in His Word Today:

A promise to believe,
a warning to heed, a command to obey,
encouragement to receive,
or wisdom to understand.

My Prayer

My Day

My Plans

Begin your Quiet Time with Prayer

Jesus said to him,

"I am the way, the truth, and the life.

No one comes to the Father except through Me.

John 14:6

My Bible Reading Plan for Today: _____

date: _____

A verse that touched my heart:

_____

_____

_____

_____

_____

_____

_____

_____

It's Bible Reading Time!

What God Showed to Me in His Word Today:

A promise to believe,
a warning to heed, a command to obey,
encouragement to receive,
or wisdom to understand.

_____

_____

_____

_____

_____

_____

_____

_____

_____

My Prayer _____

_____

_____

My Day _____

_____

_____

My Plans _____

_____

Begin your Quiet Time with Prayer

For it is the God who commanded light to shine out of darkness,
who has shone in our hearts to give
the light of the knowledge of the glory of God
in the face of Jesus Christ.
2 Corinthians 4:6

My Bible Reading Plan for Today: _____

date: _____

A verse that touched my heart:

_____

_____

_____

_____

it's Bible Reading Time!

What God Showed to Me in His Word Today:

A promise to believe,
a warning to heed, a command to obey,
encouragement to receive,
or wisdom to understand.

My Prayer

My Day

My Plans

Begin your Quiet Time with Prayer

Have you not known? Have you not heard?
The everlasting God, the LORD,
The Creator of the ends of the earth,
Neither faints nor is weary.
His understanding is unsearchable.
Isaiah 40:28

My Bible Reading Plan for Today: _____

date: _____

A verse that touched my heart:

_____

_____

_____

_____

_____

_____

_____

_____

_____

_____

it's Bible Reading Time!

What God Showed to Me in His Word Today:

A promise to believe,
a warning to heed, a command to obey,
encouragement to receive,
or wisdom to understand.

My Prayer

My Day

My Plans

Begin your Quiet Time with Prayer

Trust in Him at all times, you people;

Pour out your heart before Him;

God *is* a refuge for us.

Psalm 62:8

My Bible Reading Plan for Today: _____

date: _____

A verse that touched my heart:

it's Bible Reading Time!

What God Showed to Me in His Word Today:

A promise to believe,
a warning to heed, a command to obey,
encouragement to receive,
or wisdom to understand.

My Prayer

My Day

My Plans

Begin your Quiet Time with Prayer

And do not be conformed to this world,
but be transformed by the renewing of your mind,
that you may prove what *is* that good and acceptable
and perfect will of God.
Romans 12:2

My Bible Reading Plan for Today: _____

date: _____

A verse that touched my heart:

_____

_____

_____

_____

_____

_____

_____

_____

_____

it's Bible Reading Time!

What God Showed to Me in His Word Today:

A promise to believe,
a warning to heed, a command to obey,
encouragement to receive,
or wisdom to understand.

_____

_____

_____

_____

_____

_____

_____

_____

_____

My Prayer

_____

_____

My Day

_____

_____

My Plans

_____

_____

Four ways to bless others:

Begin your Quiet Time with Prayer

'Not by might nor by power,

but by My Spirit,'

Says the LORD of hosts.

Zechariah 4:6b

My Bible Reading Plan for Today: _____

date: _____

A verse that touched my heart:

it's Bible Reading Time!

What God Showed to Me in His Word Today:

A promise to believe,
a warning to heed, a command to obey,
encouragement to receive,
or wisdom to understand.

_____

_____

_____

_____

_____

_____

_____

_____

My Prayer _____

_____

_____

My Day _____

_____

_____

My Plans _____

_____

Begin your Quiet Time with Prayer

I will go in the strength of the Lord GOD;

I will make mention of Your righteousness,

of Yours only.

Psalm 71:16

My Bible Reading Plan for Today: _____

date: _____

A verse that touched my heart:

it's Bible Reading Time!

What God Showed to Me in His Word Today:

A promise to believe,
a warning to heed, a command to obey,
encouragement to receive,
or wisdom to understand.

My Prayer

My Day

My Plans

Begin your Quiet Time with Prayer

The fear of the LORD *is* the beginning of wisdom,
And the knowledge of the Holy One *is* understanding.

Proverbs 9:10

My Bible Reading Plan for Today: _____

date: _____

A verse that touched my heart:

_____

_____

_____

_____

_____

_____

_____

_____

it's Bible Reading Time!

What God Showed to Me in His Word Today:

A promise to believe,
a warning to heed, a command to obey,
encouragement to receive,
or wisdom to understand.

My Prayer

My Day

My Plans

Begin your Quiet Time with Prayer

Therefore, as the elect of God, holy and beloved,
put on tender mercies, kindness,
humility, meekness, longsuffering.
Colossians 3:12

My Bible Reading Plan for Today: _____

date: _____

A verse that touched my heart:

it's Bible Reading Time!

What God Showed to Me in His Word Today:

A promise to believe,
a warning to heed, a command to obey,
encouragement to receive,
or wisdom to understand.

My Prayer

My Day

My Plans

Begin your Quiet Time with Prayer

The LORD has appeared of old to me, saying:
"Yes, I have loved you with an everlasting love;
Therefore with loving-kindness I have drawn you.
Jeremiah 31:3

My Bible Reading Plan for Today: _____

date: _____

A verse that touched my heart:

it's Bible Reading Time!

What God Showed to Me in His Word Today:

A promise to believe,
a warning to heed, a command to obey,
encouragement to receive,
or wisdom to understand.

_____

_____

_____

_____

_____

_____

_____

_____

My Prayer

_____

_____

My Day

_____

_____

My Plans

_____

Begin your Quiet Time with Prayer

When Christ who is our life appears,
then you also will appear with Him in glory.
Colossians 3:4

My Bible Reading Plan for Today: _____

date: _____

A verse that touched my heart:

It's Bible Reading Time!

What God Showed to Me in His Word Today:

A promise to believe,
a warning to heed, a command to obey,
encouragement to receive,
or wisdom to understand.

My Prayer

My Day

My Plans

Begin your Quiet Time with Prayer

But let him who glories glory in this,
That he understands and knows Me,
That I am the LORD, exercising lovingkindness,
judgment, and righteousness in the earth.
For in these I delight," says the LORD.
Jeremiah 9:24

My Bible Reading Plan for Today: _____

date: _____

A verse that touched my heart:

_____

_____

_____

_____

_____

_____

_____

_____

it's Bible Reading Time!

What God Showed to Me in His Word Today:

A promise to believe,
a warning to heed, a command to obey,
encouragement to receive,
or wisdom to understand.

My Prayer

My Day

My Plans

Four reasons to be joyful:

Begin your Quiet Time with Prayer

I beseech you therefore, brethren,
by the mercies of God,
that you present your bodies a living sacrifice, holy,
acceptable to God, *which is* your reasonable service.
Romans 12:1

My Bible Reading Plan for Today: _____

date: _____

A verse that touched my heart:

it's Bible Reading Time!

What God Showed to Me in His Word Today:

A promise to believe,
a warning to heed, a command to obey,
encouragement to receive,
or wisdom to understand.

My Prayer

My Day

My Plans

Begin your Quiet Time with Prayer

Greater love has no one than this,

than to lay down one's life

for his friends.

John 15:13

My Bible Reading Plan for Today: _____

date: _____

A verse that touched my heart:

_____

_____

_____

_____

_____

_____

_____

_____

_____

_____

_____

it's Bible Reading Time!

What God Showed to Me in His Word Today:

A promise to believe,
a warning to heed, a command to obey,
encouragement to receive,
or wisdom to understand.

My Prayer

My Day

My Plans

Begin your Quiet Time with Prayer

But God demonstrates His own love toward us,
in that while we were still sinners, Christ died for us.
Romans 5:8

My Bible Reading Plan for Today: _____

date: _____

A verse that touched my heart:

It's Bible Reading Time!

What God Showed to Me in His Word Today

A promise to believe,
a warning to heed, a command to obey,
encouragement to receive,
or wisdom to understand.

_____

_____

_____

_____

_____

_____

_____

_____

My Prayer _____

_____

_____

My Day _____

_____

My Plans _____

_____

Begin your Quiet Time with Prayer

For as the heavens are high above the earth,
So great is His mercy toward those who fear Him;
As far as the east is from the west,
So far has He removed our transgressions from us.
Psalm 103:11-12

My Bible Reading Plan for Today: _____

date: _____

A verse that touched my heart:

it's Bible Reading Time!

What God Showed to Me in His Word Today:

A promise to believe,
a warning to heed, a command to obey,
encouragement to receive,
or wisdom to understand.

My Prayer

My Day

My Plans

Begin your Quiet Time with Prayer

In the beginning God
created the heavens and the earth.
Genesis 1:1

My Bible Reading Plan for Today: _____

date: _____

A verse that touched my heart:

_____

_____

_____

_____

_____

_____

_____

_____

_____

it's Bible Reading Time!

What God Showed to Me in His Word Today:

A promise to believe,
a warning to heed, a command to obey,
encouragement to receive,
or wisdom to understand.

_____

_____

_____

_____

_____

_____

_____

My Prayer

_____

_____

My Day

_____

_____

My Plans

_____

_____

Begin your Quiet Time with Prayer

While we do not look at the things which are seen,
but at the things which are not seen.
For the things which are seen are temporary,
but the things which are not seen are eternal.
2 Corinthians 4:18

My Bible Reading Plan for Today: _____

date: _____

A verse that touched my heart:

it's Bible Reading Time!

What God Showed to Me in His Word Today:

A promise to believe,
a warning to heed, a command to obey,
encouragement to receive,
or wisdom to understand.

My Prayer

My Day

My Plans

Begin your Quiet Time with Prayer

I am the vine, you are the branches.

He who abides in Me, and I in him, bears much fruit;

for without Me you can do nothing.

John 15:5

My Bible Reading Plan for Today: _____

date: _____

A verse that touched my heart:

it's Bible Reading Time!

What God Showed to Me in His Word Today:

A promise to believe,
a warning to heed, a command to obey,
encouragement to receive,
or wisdom to understand.

My Prayer

My Day

My Plans

Four promises from the Bible:

Begin your Quiet Time with Prayer

Your word was to me the joy
and rejoicing of my heart;
For I am called by Your name,
O LORD God of hosts.
Jeremiah 15:16b

My Bible Reading Plan for Today: _____

date: _____

A verse that touched my heart:

_____

_____

_____

_____

_____

_____

_____

_____

_____

it's Bible Reading Time!

What God Showed to Me in His Word Today:

A promise to believe,
a warning to heed, a command to obey,
encouragement to receive,
or wisdom to understand.

My Prayer

My Day

My Plans

Begin your Quiet Time with Prayer

Return to your rest, O my soul,

For the LORD has dealt bountifully with you.

For You have delivered my soul from death,

My eyes from tears,

And my feet from falling.

Psalm 116:7-8

My Bible Reading Plan for Today: _____

date: _____

A verse that touched my heart:

_____

_____

_____

_____

_____

_____

_____

_____

it's Bible Reading Time!

What God Showed to Me in His Word Today:

A promise to believe,
a warning to heed, a command to obey,
encouragement to receive,
or wisdom to understand.

My Prayer

My Day

My Plans

Begin your Quiet Time with Prayer

The LORD is my shepherd;

I shall not want.

Psalm 23:1

My Bible Reading Plan for Today: _____

date: _____

A verse that touched my heart:

it's Bible Reading Time!

What God Showed to Me in His Word Today:

A promise to believe,
a warning to heed, a command to obey,
encouragement to receive,
or wisdom to understand.

My Prayer

My Day

My Plans

Begin your Quiet Time with Prayer

For our citizenship is in heaven,

from which we also eagerly wait for the Savior,

the Lord Jesus Christ

Philippians 3:20

My Bible Reading Plan for Today: _____

date: _____

A verse that touched my heart:

it's Bible Reading Time!

What God Showed to Me in His Word Today:

A promise to believe,
a warning to heed, a command to obey,
encouragement to receive,
or wisdom to understand.

My Prayer

My Day

My Plans

Begin your Quiet Time with Prayer

Come to Me,

all you who labor and are heavy laden,

and I will give you rest.

Matthew 11:28

My Bible Reading Plan for Today: _____

date: _____

A verse that touched my heart:

_____

_____

_____

_____

_____

_____

_____

_____

_____

it's Bible Reading Time!

What God Showed to Me in His Word Today:

A promise to believe,
a warning to heed, a command to obey,
encouragement to receive,
or wisdom to understand.

My Prayer

My Day

My Plans

Begin your Quiet Time with Prayer

Fear not, for I am with you;
Be not dismayed, for I am your God.
I will strengthen you, yes, I will help you,
I will uphold you with My righteous right hand.
Isaiah 41:10

My Bible Reading Plan for Today: _____
date: _____

A verse that touched my heart:

_____

_____

_____

_____

_____

_____

_____

_____

it's Bible Reading Time!

What God Showed to Me in His Word Today:

A promise to believe,
a warning to heed, a command to obey,
encouragement to receive,
or wisdom to understand.

My Prayer

My Day

My Plans

Begin your Quiet Time with Prayer

You will show me the path of life;
In Your presence *is* fullness of joy;
At Your right hand *are* pleasures forevermore.
Psalm 16:11

My Bible Reading Plan for Today: _____

date: _____

A verse that touched my heart:

it's Bible Reading Time!

What God Showed to Me in His Word Today:

A promise to believe,
a warning to heed, a command to obey,
encouragement to receive,
or wisdom to understand.

My Prayer

My Day

My Plans

Four ways to bless others:

Begin your Quiet Time with Prayer

Fulfill my joy by being like-minded,

having the same love,

being of one accord, of one mind.

Philippians 2:2

My Bible Reading Plan for Today: _____

date: _____

A verse that touched my heart:

it's Bible Reading Time!

What God Showed to Me in His Word Today:

A promise to believe,
a warning to heed, a command to obey,
encouragement to receive,
or wisdom to understand.

My Prayer

My Day

My Plans

Begin your Quiet Time with Prayer

But seek first the kingdom of God
and His righteousness,
and all these things shall be added to you.
Matthew 6:33

My Bible Reading Plan for Today: _____

date: _____

A verse that touched my heart:

_____

_____

_____

_____

_____

_____

_____

_____

_____

It's Bible Reading Time!

What God Showed to Me in His Word Today:

A promise to believe,
a warning to heed, a command to obey,
encouragement to receive,
or wisdom to understand.

My Prayer

My Day

My Plans

Begin your Quiet Time with Prayer

For all have sinned
and fall short of the glory of God,
being justified freely by His grace
through the redemption that is in Christ Jesus.
Romans 3:23-24

My Bible Reading Plan for Today: _____

date: _____

A verse that touched my heart:

it's Bible Reading Time!

What God Showed to Me in His Word Today:

A promise to believe,
a warning to heed, a command to obe
encouragement to receive,
or wisdom to understand.

_____

_____

_____

_____

_____

_____

_____

_____

My Prayer

_____

_____

_____

My Day

_____

_____

My Plans

_____

_____

Begin your Quiet Time with Prayer

But Jesus looked at them and said to them,
"With men this is impossible,
but with God all things are possible."
Matthew 19:26

My Bible Reading Plan for Today: _____

date: _____

A verse that touched my heart:

_____

_____

_____

_____

_____

_____

_____

_____

_____

_____

_____

it's Bible Reading Time!

What God Showed to Me in His Word Today:

A promise to believe,
a warning to heed, a command to obey,
encouragement to receive,
or wisdom to understand.

My Prayer

My Day

My Plans

Begin your Quiet Time with Prayer

Therefore, if anyone is in Christ,
he is a new creation;
old things have passed away;
behold, all things have become new.
2 Corinthians 5:17

My Bible Reading Plan for Today: _____

date: _____

A verse that touched my heart:

it's Bible Reading Time!

What God Showed to Me in His Word Today:

A promise to believe,
a warning to heed, a command to obey,
encouragement to receive,
or wisdom to understand.

My Prayer

My Day

My Plans

Begin your Quiet Time with Prayer

But those who wait on the LORD
Shall renew *their* strength;
They shall mount up with wings like eagles,
They shall run and not be weary,
They shall walk and not faint.

Isaiah 40:31

My Bible Reading Plan for Today: _____

date: _____

A verse that touched my heart:

_____

_____

_____

_____

_____

_____

_____

_____

_____

_____

it's Bible Reading Time!

What God Showed to Me in His Word Today:

A promise to believe,
a warning to heed, a command to obey,
encouragement to receive,
or wisdom to understand.

My Prayer

My Day

My Plans

Begin your Quiet Time with Prayer

What shall I render to the LORD
For all His benefits toward me?
I will take up the cup of salvation,
And call upon the name of the LORD.
Psalm 116:12-13

My Bible Reading Plan for Today: _____

date: _____

A verse that touched my heart:

it's Bible Reading Time!

What God Showed to Me in His Word Today:

A promise to believe,
a warning to heed, a command to obey,
encouragement to receive,
or wisdom to understand.

My Prayer

My Day

My Plans

Four reasons to be thankful:

Begin your Quiet Time with Prayer

For I am not ashamed of the gospel of Christ,

for it is the power of God to salvation

for everyone who believes,

Romans 1:16a

My Bible Reading Plan for Today: _____

date: _____

A verse that touched my heart:

it's Bible Reading Time!

What God Showed to Me in His Word Today:

A promise to believe,
a warning to heed, a command to obey,
encouragement to receive,
or wisdom to understand.

My Prayer

My Day

My Plans

Begin your Quiet Time with Prayer

Remember the word that I said to you,
'A servant is not greater than his master.'
If they persecuted Me, they will also persecute you.
If they kept My word, they will keep yours also.
John 15:20

My Bible Reading Plan for Today: _____

date: _____

A verse that touched my heart:

_____

_____

_____

_____

_____

_____

_____

_____

_____

it's Bible Reading Time!

What God Showed to Me in His Word Today:

A promise to believe,
a warning to heed, a command to obey,
encouragement to receive,
or wisdom to understand.

My Prayer

My Day

My Plans

Begin your Quiet Time with Prayer

For the word of God is living and powerful,
and sharper than any two-edged sword,
piercing even to the division of soul and spirit, and of joints and marrow,
and is a discerner of the thoughts and intents of the heart.
Hebrews 4:12

My Bible Reading Plan for Today: _____

date: _____

A verse that touched my heart:

_____

_____

_____

_____

_____

_____

_____

_____

_____

it's Bible Reading Time!

What God Showed to Me in His Word Today:

A promise to believe,
a warning to heed, a command to obey,
encouragement to receive,
or wisdom to understand.

My Prayer

My Day

My Plans

Begin your Quiet Time with Prayer

Jesus said to her,

"I am the resurrection and the life.

He who believes in Me, though he may die, he shall live.

John 11:25

My Bible Reading Plan for Today: _____

date: _____

A verse that touched my heart:

_____

_____

_____

_____

_____

_____

_____

_____

it's Bible Reading Time!

What God Showed to Me in His Word Today:

A promise to believe,
a warning to heed, a command to obey,
encouragement to receive,
or wisdom to understand.

My Prayer

My Day

My Plans

Begin your Quiet Time with Prayer

He has shown you, O man, what is good;
And what does the LORD require of you
But to do justly, to love mercy,
And to walk humbly with your God?
Micah 6:8

My Bible Reading Plan for Today: _____

date: _____

A verse that touched my heart:

it's Bible Reading Time!

What God Showed to Me in His Word Today:

A promise to believe,
a warning to heed, a command to obey,
encouragement to receive,
or wisdom to understand.

My Prayer

My Day

My Plans

Begin your Quiet Time with Prayer

Open my eyes, that I may see
wondrous things from Your law.
Psalm119:18

My Bible Reading Plan for Today: _____

date: _____

A verse that touched my heart:

it's Bible Reading Time!

What God Showed to Me in His Word Today:

A promise to believe,
a warning to heed, a command to obey,
encouragement to receive,
or wisdom to understand.

My Prayer

My Day

My Plans

Begin your Quiet Time with Prayer

Behold what manner of love
the Father has bestowed on us,
that we should be called children of God!
I John 3:1a

My Bible Reading Plan for Today: _____

date: _____

A verse that touched my heart:

_____

_____

_____

_____

_____

_____

_____

_____

it's Bible Reading Time!

What God Showed to Me in His Word Today:

A promise to believe,
a warning to heed, a command to obey,
encouragement to receive,
or wisdom to understand.

My Prayer

My Day

My Plans

Four dreams for my future:

Begin your Quiet Time with Prayer

Then Jesus said to those Jews who believed Him,
"If you abide in My word, you are My disciples indeed.
And you shall know the truth,
and the truth shall make you free."
John 8:31-32

My Bible Reading Plan for Today: _____
date: _____

A verse that touched my heart:

it's Bible Reading Time!

What God Showed to Me in His Word Today:

A promise to believe,
a warning to heed, a command to obey,
encouragement to receive,
or wisdom to understand.

My Prayer

My Day

My Plans

Begin your Quiet Time with Prayer

When You said, "Seek My face,"

My heart said to You,

"Your face, LORD, I will seek."

Psalm 27:8

My Bible Reading Plan for Today: _____

date: _____

A verse that touched my heart:

it's Bible Reading Time!

What God Showed to Me in His Word Today:

A promise to believe,
a warning to heed, a command to obey,
encouragement to receive,
or wisdom to understand.

My Prayer

My Day

My Plans

Begin your Quiet Time with Prayer

Let the word of Christ dwell in you richly
in all wisdom, teaching and admonishing one another
in psalms and hymns and spiritual songs,
singing with grace in your hearts to the Lord.
Colossians 3:16

My Bible Reading Plan for Today: _____

date: _____

A verse that touched my heart:

_____

_____

_____

_____

it's Bible Reading Time!

What God Showed to Me in His Word Today:

A promise to believe,
a warning to heed, a command to obey,
encouragement to receive,
or wisdom to understand.

My Prayer

My Day

My Plans

Begin your Quiet Time with Prayer

Finally, brethren, whatever things are true, whatever things are noble,
whatever things are just, whatever things are pure,
whatever things are lovely, whatever things are of good report,
If there is any virtue and if there is anything praiseworthy—
meditate on these things.

Philippians 4:8

My Bible Reading Plan for Today: _____

date: _____

A verse that touched my heart:

it's Bible Reading Time!

What God Showed to Me in His Word Today

A promise to believe,
a warning to heed, a command to obey
encouragement to receive,
or wisdom to understand.

_____

_____

_____

_____

_____

_____

_____

_____

My Prayer _____

_____

_____

My Day _____

_____

My Plans _____

_____

Begin your Quiet Time with Prayer

These things I have spoken to you,
that in Me you may have peace.
In the world you will have tribulation;
but be of good cheer, I have overcome the world.
John 16:33

My Bible Reading Plan for Today: _____

date: _____

A verse that touched my heart:

It's Bible Reading Time!

What God Showed to Me in His Word Today:

A promise to believe,
a warning to heed, a command to obey,
encouragement to receive,
or wisdom to understand.

My Prayer

My Day

My Plans

Begin your Quiet Time with Prayer

Before the mountains were brought forth,
Or ever You had formed the earth and the world,
Even from everlasting to everlasting,
You are God.
Psalm 90:2

My Bible Reading Plan for Today: _____

date: _____

A verse that touched my heart:

It's Bible Reading Time!

What God Showed to Me in His Word Today:

A promise to believe,
a warning to heed, a command to obey,
encouragement to receive,
or wisdom to understand.

My Prayer

My Day

My Plans

Begin your Quiet Time with Prayer

For you have need of endurance, so that after you have done the
will of God, you may receive the promise.
Hebrews 10:36

My Bible Reading Plan for Today: _____

date: _____

A verse that touched my heart:

it's Bible Reading Time!

What God Showed to Me in His Word Today:

A promise to believe,
a warning to heed, a command to obey,
encouragement to receive,
or wisdom to understand.

_____

_____

_____

_____

_____

_____

_____

_____

My Prayer

_____

_____

_____

My Day

_____

_____

My Plans

_____

_____

Four goals for next week:

Begin your Quiet Time with Prayer

But you, when you pray, go into your room,
and when you have shut your door,
pray to your Father who is in the secret place;
and your Father who sees in secret will reward you openly.
Matthew 6:6

My Bible Reading Plan for Today: _____

date: _____

A verse that touched my heart:

it's Bible Reading Time!

What God Showed to Me in His Word Today:

A promise to believe,
a warning to heed, a command to obey,
encouragement to receive,
or wisdom to understand.

My Prayer

My Day

My Plans

Begin your Quiet Time with Prayer

But when the Helper comes,

whom I shall send to you from the Father,

the Spirit of truth who proceeds from the Father,

He will testify of Me.

John 15:26

My Bible Reading Plan for Today: _____

date: _____

A verse that touched my heart:

it's Bible Reading Time!

What God Showed to Me in His Word Today:

A promise to believe,
a warning to heed, a command to obey,
encouragement to receive,
or wisdom to understand.

My Prayer

My Day

My Plans

Begin your Quiet Time with Prayer

So Jesus said to them again,

"Peace to you!

As the Father has sent Me,

I also send you."

John 20:21

My Bible Reading Plan for Today: _____

date: _____

A verse that touched my heart:

_____

_____

_____

_____

_____

_____

_____

_____

it's Bible Reading Time!

What God Showed to Me in His Word Today:

A promise to believe,
a warning to heed, a command to obey,
encouragement to receive,
or wisdom to understand.

_____

_____

_____

_____

_____

_____

_____

_____

My Prayer

_____

_____

_____

My Day

_____

_____

My Plans

_____

_____

Begin your Quiet Time with Prayer

And this is His commandment:

that we should believe on the name of His Son Jesus Christ and

love one another, as He gave us commandment.

I John 3:23

My Bible Reading Plan for Today: _____

date: _____

A verse that touched my heart:

it's Bible Reading Time!

What God Showed to Me in His Word Today:

A promise to believe,
a warning to heed, a command to obey,
encouragement to receive,
or wisdom to understand.

My Prayer

My Day

My Plans

Begin your Quiet Time with Prayer

Praise the LORD!

For it is good to sing praises to our God;

For it is pleasant, and praise is beautiful.

Psalm 147:1

My Bible Reading Plan for Today: _____

date: _____

A verse that touched my heart:

it's Bible Reading Time!

What God Showed to Me in His Word Today:

A promise to believe,
a warning to heed, a command to obey,
encouragement to receive,
or wisdom to understand.

My Prayer

My Day

My Plans

Begin your Quiet Time with Prayer

God *is* our refuge and strength,
A very present help in trouble.
Psalm 46:1

My Bible Reading Plan for Today: _____

date: _____

A verse that touched my heart:

it's Bible Reading Time!

What God Showed to Me in His Word Today:

A promise to believe,
a warning to heed, a command to obey,
encouragement to receive,
or wisdom to understand.

My Prayer

My Day

My Plans

Begin your Quiet Time with Prayer

For all the law is fulfilled in one word,

even in this:

"You shall love your neighbor as yourself."

Galatians 5:14

My Bible Reading Plan for Today: _____

date: _____

A verse that touched my heart:

it's Bible Reading Time!

What God Showed to Me in His Word Today:

A promise to believe,
a warning to heed, a command to obey,
encouragement to receive,
or wisdom to understand.

My Prayer

My Day

My Plans

Four people to pray for:

Begin your Quiet Time with Prayer

If anyone serves Me, let him follow Me;
and where I am, there My servant will be also.
If anyone serves Me, him My Father will honor.
John 12:26

My Bible Reading Plan for Today: _____

date: _____

A verse that touched my heart:

it's Bible Reading Time!

What God Showed to Me in His Word Today:

A promise to believe,
a warning to heed, a command to obey,
encouragement to receive,
or wisdom to understand.

_____

_____

_____

_____

_____

_____

_____

_____

_____

My Prayer

_____

_____

_____

My Day

_____

_____

My Plans

_____

_____

Begin your Quiet Time with Prayer

Thus says the LORD: "Stand in the ways and see,
and ask for the old paths, where the good way is,
and walk in it; then you will find rest for your souls."
Jeremiah 6:16a

My Bible Reading Plan for Today: _____

date: _____

A verse that touched my heart:

_____

_____

_____

_____

_____

_____

_____

_____

it's Bible Reading Time!

What God Showed to Me in His Word Today:

A promise to believe,
a warning to heed, a command to obey,
encouragement to receive,
or wisdom to understand.

_____

_____

_____

_____

_____

_____

_____

_____

_____

My Prayer _____

_____

_____

My Day _____

_____

My Plans _____

_____

Begin your Quiet Time with Prayer

The LORD *is* near to all who call upon Him,

To all who call upon Him in truth.

Psalm 145:18

My Bible Reading Plan for Today: _____

date: _____

A verse that touched my heart:

_____

_____

_____

_____

_____

_____

_____

_____

_____

it's Bible Reading Time!

What God Showed to Me in His Word Today:

A promise to believe,
a warning to heed, a command to obey.
encouragement to receive,
or wisdom to understand.

_____

_____

_____

_____

_____

_____

_____

My Prayer

_____

_____

_____

My Day

_____

_____

My Plans

_____

_____

Begin your Quiet Time with Prayer

Then Jesus said to them ... The thief does not come except
to steal, and to kill, and to destroy.
I have come that they may have life,
and that they may have it more abundantly.
John 10:7a & 10

My Bible Reading Plan for Today: _____

date: _____

A verse that touched my heart:

_____

_____

_____

_____

_____

_____

_____

_____

_____

_____

it's Bible Reading Time!

What God Showed to Me in His Word Today:

A promise to believe,
a warning to heed, a command to obey,
encouragement to receive,
or wisdom to understand.

My Prayer

My Day

My Plans

Begin your Quiet Time with Prayer

Most assuredly, I say to you,
he who hears My word and believes in Him who sent Me
has everlasting life, and shall not come into judgment,
but has passed from death into life.

John 5:24

My Bible Reading Plan for Today: _____

date: _____

A verse that touched my heart:

_____

_____

_____

_____

_____

_____

_____

_____

_____

it's Bible Reading Time!

What God Showed to Me in His Word Today:

A promise to believe,
a warning to heed, a command to obey,
encouragement to receive,
or wisdom to understand.

My Prayer

My Day

My Plans

Begin your Quiet Time with Prayer

Jesus stood and cried out, saying,

"If anyone thirsts, let him come to Me and drink.

He who believes in Me, as the Scripture has said,

out of his heart will flow rivers of living water."

John 7:37b-38

My Bible Reading Plan for Today: _____

date: _____

A verse that touched my heart:

_____

_____

_____

_____

_____

_____

_____

_____

_____

_____

it's Bible Reading Time!

What God Showed to Me in His Word Today:

A promise to believe,
a warning to heed, a command to obey,
encouragement to receive,
or wisdom to understand.

My Prayer

My Day

My Plans

Four ways to serve my family:

Hi!

Now that you have completed 90 days of time alone with the Lord, reading His word, listening to hear the voice of the Holy Spirit whispering to your heart the things He wants to tell you, keep listening. Read your Bible and expect for God to speak to you, and be ready to write down the promise, or encouragement, command, or words of wisdom.

All you need now is your Bible, a journal with nothing written on the pages. And don't forget a cozy quiet place, and perhaps, a cup of tea, and your favorite worship music too.

If you enjoy coloring during your quiet time, look for our other devotional coloring books.

Blessings Always,
    Georgia

Made in the USA
Coppell, TX
20 February 2022